This is no longer
property of
King County Library System

AUG 1 6 2009
REDMOND REGIONAL LIBRARY

KING COUNTY LIBRARY SYSTEM, WA

IN THEIR OWN WORDS

Dear Sally,

I just wanted to
that everything's ok w
your family. We wat
horror the collapse of
World Trade Center.
awful. I can't believ
you were working in th
New York when it l
world has changed
a short space of time

SEPTEMBER 11
A Primary Source History

Alan Wachtel

Gareth Stevens
Publishing

KING COUNTY LIBRARY SYSTEM, WA

KEY TO SYMBOLS

Look out for the following symbols through this book, highlighting key articles from the past.

FILM EXCERPT *Primary source material from a film about the subject matter.*

GOVERNMENT DOCUMENT *Text extracted from an official government document.*

INTERVIEW/BOOK EXTRACT *Text from an interview or a book.*

SONG/POEM *Text from songs or poems about the subject matter.*

LETTER *Text from a letter written by a participant in the events.*

NEWSPAPER ARTICLE *Extracts from newspapers of the period.*

OFFICIAL SPEECH *Transcribed words from official government speeches.*

PLAQUE/INSCRIPTION *Text taken from plaques or monuments erected in memory of events described in this book.*

TELEGRAM *Text from a telegram sent to or by a participant in the events.*

TELEPHONE *Text taken from a phone call.*

E-MAIL *Text taken from an email sent to or by a participant in the events.*

Cover photos:
Top left: A firefighter weeps on September 11, 2001.
Top right: A letter to a person who was working in the World Trade Center during the 9/11 attacks.
Background: A U.S. flag is posted in the rubble of the World Trade Center September 13, 2001, in New York.

CONTENTS

Above: *Before the attacks of 9/11, the Twin Towers of the World Trade Center were the tallest buildings in New York City.*

Above: *Located in Arlington, Virginia, the Pentagon is the headquarters of the United States Department of Defense.*

*S*eptember 11, 2001, was one of the single most shocking and tragic days in the history of the United States. When 19 terrorists hijacked four U.S. passenger planes that morning, they unleashed a wave of death, injury, destruction, and fear within the space of only a few hours. Approximately 3,000 lives were lost that day. No act of war by a foreign power had ever caused that many lives to be lost on U.S. soil.

People were stunned when the first hijacked plane flew into the North Tower of the World Trade Center (WTC). Within minutes, live televised images of the burning skyscraper were breaking into the morning news. Many believed it must have been an accident. Minutes later, millions watched in horror as a second plane hit the South Tower. As a third plane hit the Pentagon—the headquarters of the U.S. armed forces—outside Washington, D.C., and a fourth crashed in a field in Pennsylvania, few believed this could be anything but an attack on the United States.

The attacks of September 11, 2001, have become part of American history. The story of September 11, 2001, is more than just the tale of one terrible day. It is the story of the many ways the United States and its allies have responded to the threat of terrorism. It is the story of how the United States—its people and its government—has responded to the attacks, mourned lost lives, and moved forward.

The World Trade Center was built in the 1970s. It was a group of seven buildings in downtown Manhattan. Hundreds of companies from all over the world rented space in the buildings. The Twin Towers were the most famous buildings of the group. At 110 stories tall, they stood out in the New York City skyline. To some, they were symbols not only of New York City but also of the leading role of the United States in the international economy.

Less than two hours after the hijacked planes struck them, the Twin Towers collapsed. There was also a huge hole in the west wall of the Pentagon. Investigators believe terrorists planned to fly the fourth aircraft, which crashed into a field in Pennsylvania, into either the U.S. Capitol or the White House.

The perpetrators of the horrific attacks were believed to be members of al-Qaeda led by Osama bin Laden. Until September 11th, most Americans did not know who bin Laden was. Soon after the attacks, the faces of bin Laden and the hijackers were all over the media. So were the faces of the thousands of victims. In the months following the attacks, the nations of the world rallied to support the United States. The United States demanded that Afghanistan, the country that was believed to be sheltering bin Laden and al-Qaeda, turn over the terrorist leader. When the leaders of Afghanistan

Above: *The west wall of the Pentagon was seriously damaged and 125 people were killed when terrorists crashed American Airlines Flight 77 into the building on September 11, 2001.*

Below: *Osama bin Laden, head of the terrorist group al-Qaeda, took credit for the attack.*

Above: *United Airlines Flight 175 before it hit the South Tower of the World Trade Center. The North Tower burns after being hit by American Airlines Flight 11.*

refused, the United States and an international coalition invaded Afghanistan to capture bin Laden and overthrow the Taliban for harboring al-Qaeda.

At about the same time, the fear of terrorism brought dramatic changes within the United States. Security increased dramatically at nearly every target terrorists might want to attack. Airport security increased. Concrete barriers were placed near tall buildings so that car bombs could not be driven into them. Police guarded important public works, such as dams. The government passed a number of laws to help keep people safe. These laws led to a controversy over whether these new government powers harmed the civil liberties of Americans. The U.S. government also found itself facing criticism at home and abroad over some of its responses to the attacks, including the decision to send military troops into Iraq in 2003.

In November 2002, the U.S. government set up the National Commission on Terrorist Attacks, also known as the "9/11 Commission." Commission members studied the events to try to tell the story of what happened during the attacks. They also studied the historic events that led up to 9/11 and the question of whether the attacks could have been prevented. Finally, commission members gave recommendations on how to deal with the future threat of terrorism. Their work took almost two years. In July 2004, their final report was released.

Below: *Air Force soldiers from the United States, Great Britain, and Australia work together as part of Operation Iraqi Freedom in 2003.*

In the years since the attacks, every anniversary of 9/11 has been marked by mourning and remembrance. A constant stream of books, articles, and editorials discusses the effect of September 11 on the United States and the world, whether the terrorist plot could have been stopped, and how to best prevent future attacks by terrorists. Movies have been made about terrorism, the attacks themselves, and the victims. Artists and musicians have also addressed the attacks and their effects. Memorials have been built to make sure the victims will not be forgotten. In 2006, work began on rebuilding the site where the Twin Towers had stood. Freedom Tower, a new and even taller skyscraper, began rising out of the ruins of Ground Zero.

Above: *Construction site at Ground Zero, where the new Freedom Tower will reside.*

Right: *The Sphere, a statue by Fritz Koenig, was damaged by the 9/11 terrorist attacks. Before the attacks, it stood between the Twin Towers. It now stands in New York City's Battery Park as part of a memorial to the victims of the attacks.*

The morning of September 11th, 2001, was a seemingly perfect day. The sky was clear and cloudless—conditions for air travel could not have been better. But the morning would turn tragic.

Above: *An airport security official checks through passengers' luggage. Following the attacks of 9/11, security checks have become more detailed.*

Below: *Before September 11, the Twin Towers rose higher than the other buildings in the New York City skyline.*

THE TWIN TOWERS

In New York City's World Trade Center, people began arriving for work. About 50,000 people worked in the Twin Towers each day. In addition to these employees, about 40,000 others visited the buildings daily. The visitors included a wide variety of businesspeople, delivery people, and tourists from both near and far who came to look out across New York from the observation decks of the tallest buildings in the city.

From their location in lower Manhattan, the Twin Towers had been the focus of the skyline of New York City since their completion in the 1970s. Each tower had 110 stories and stood about 1,365 feet (416 meters) high.

TEAMS OF TERRORISTS

At airports, passengers checked in, passed through security, and boarded their flights. Among these fliers, however, were 19 male terrorists. Some of the men were pulled aside while going through security and questioned. They were checked with metal-detection wands and their bags were tested for explosives. Never imagining the terrorists' true purpose, the security officials simply held aside the mens' bags until officials knew the men had boarded their planes. Otherwise, the hijackers boarded their flights like ordinary travelers.

At Logan International Airport, in Boston, Massachusetts, five terrorists boarded American Airlines Flight 11, headed for Los Angeles, California. At about the same time, at another gate in Logan, five more terrorists boarded United Airlines Flight 175, which was also headed for Los Angeles. At Dulles International Airport, located in the suburbs of Washington, D.C., another group of five terrorists took their seats on American Airlines Flight 77. This flight was also bound for Los Angeles. Finally, at Newark International Airport, in New Jersey, four terrorists boarded United Airlines Flight 93, headed for San Francisco, California. Each of the

Above: *An airport video camera captured this picture of two of the 9/11 hijackers before they boarded a plane at Dulles International Airport, in Washington, D.C.*

TIME LINE 1998-2001

AUGUST 7, 1998
Al-Qaeda attacks U.S. embassies in Kenya and Tanzania.

AUGUST 20, 1998
The United States fires missiles at an al-Qaeda camp in Afghanistan and a chemical-weapons factory in Sudan.

OCTOBER 12, 2000
Al-Qaeda attacks the USS *Cole*.

JULY 10, 2001
FBI office in Phoenix, Arizona, sends a memo warning of a plot by Osama bin Laden to train terrorist pilots.

AUGUST 6, 2001
President Bush's daily brief warns, "bin Laden Determined to Strike in U.S."

AUGUST 15, 2001
FBI agents in Minnesota investigate flight student Zacarias Moussaoui on suspicion of terrorism. They arrest him for immigration violations but do not investigate further.

airplanes that the hijackers boarded was a passenger jetliner, carrying dozens of travelers. Each airplane was also filled with the thousands of gallons of jet fuel needed for a transcontinental flight.

THE NORTH TOWER IS HIT

American Airlines Flight 11 took off just before 8 A.M. Less than 15 minutes after takeoff, the hijacking began. Flight 11 quickly lost contact with air-traffic controllers, went off course, and flew into the airspace of another flight. Shortly after the hijacking began, American Airlines received cellphone calls from flight attendants Betty Ong and Madeline "Amy" Sweeney describing the hijacking. Two terrorists who were seated in the first-class section, toward the front of the plane, stabbed two flight attendants and forced their way into the cockpit. They quickly turned off the plane's transponder, making it difficult for air-traffic controllers to monitor where the craft was on radar. At about the same time, another terrorist stabbed a passenger who is believed to have been trying to stop the hijacking. The hijackers claimed they had a bomb and sprayed either Mace or pepper spray to force the passengers to the back of the plane.

Within minutes, the hijackers had control of the plane. At about 8:25 A.M., air traffic controllers —as well as some pilots on other

"My name is Betty Ong. I'm No. 3 on Flight 11. ... The cockpit is not answering their phone. There's somebody stabbed in business class, and we can't breathe in business. Um, I think there is some Mace or something. We can't breathe. I don't know, but I think we're getting hijacked."

Extracts from a phone call from Betty Ong, flight attendant on American Airlines Flight 11, to American Airlines Southeast Reservation Center, as recorded in the FBI transcripts.

"This is Amy Sweeney ... listen, and listen to me very carefully ... I'm on Flight 11—this plane has been hijacked. ... We are flying very very low. We are flying way too low. ... Oh, my God! ... I see the water. I see the buildings."

Excerpts from flight attendant Madeline "Amy" Sweeney's call to Michael Woodward, American Airlines Flight Service Manager, during the final moments of Flight 11, compiled from sources using Woodward's notes.

Below: *This New York City firefighter was among the rescue workers at the World Trade Center.*

planes—heard an ominous message from the hijackers of Flight 11: "We have some planes. Just stay quiet, and you'll be okay. We are returning to the airport." The terrorists probably wanted the message to be heard only by the people on the plane. Not knowing how to work the equipment, they accidentally broadcast it to air traffic controllers and pilots of other planes. Hearing it, the controllers knew Flight 11 was in serious trouble.

As Ong and Sweeney described the scene on Flight 11 to American Airlines officials on the ground, they gave authorities the seat numbers of as many of the terrorists as they could. Both Ong and Sweeney said that the plane was flying dangerously, and that they could not communicate with anyone in the cockpit. The crew and passengers of Flight 11 knew their plane had

been hijacked, but they had no idea where they were headed. Sweeney was able to stay on the phone with Michael Woodward, an American Airlines manager. At about 8:44 A.M., she told him that the plane was descending quickly and flying too low. Minutes later, Flight 11 slammed into the North Tower of the World Trade Center, causing a massive explosion and killing everyone on the plane and many in the tower.

THE SOUTH TOWER IS HIT

At about the same time the Flight 11 hijackers crashed the plane into the North Tower, the team of hijackers aboard United Airlines Flight 175 took over the plane. According to reports from those aboard Flight 175, the hijacking was similar to that of Flight 11. Passengers and crew members were stabbed, the passengers were forced to the back of the plane with Mace and threatened with a bomb, and the cockpit was taken over by a terrorist pilot. Air traffic controllers did not even suspect that Flight 175 was hijacked until the plane's beacon codes suddenly began changing. When the plane went off course and could not be reached on the radio, they knew there was trouble aboard another flight. At about 8:52 A.M., passengers on the plane began calling family members, and a flight attendant called United Airlines offices. No one aboard Flight 175 seemed to know about the fate of

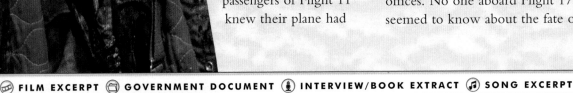

🎞️ FILM EXCERPT 📄 GOVERNMENT DOCUMENT 🎙️ INTERVIEW/BOOK EXTRACT 🎵 SONG EXCERPT

Above: *This sequence of photographs shows the attack on the South Tower. Flight 175 can be seen approaching in the top left image. This happened in a matter of seconds.*

7:59 A.M.
American Airlines Flight 11 takes off from Logan International Airport, Boston.

8:14 A.M.
United Airlines Flight 175 takes off, also from Logan International Airport.

8:20 A.M.
American Airlines Flight 77 takes off from Dulles International Airport in Washington, D.C.

Flight 11. At 9:03 A.M., Flight 175 crashed into the South Tower of the World Trade Center.

THE PENTAGON IS HIT
At about the same time that air traffic controllers were figuring out that United Flight 175 had also been hijacked, another team of terrorists took over American Airlines Flight 77 out of Washington, D.C. Phone calls from onboard Flight 77 reported that the hijackers forced them to the back of the plane with knives and box cutters. By 8:54 A.M., however, it was clear that Flight 77

was in trouble. The terrorists had shut off the plane's transponder and turned it back toward Washington. Air traffic controllers tracked Flight 77 as best they could, but with two hijacked planes in the air and a major crisis on their hands,

"It's getting bad, Dad. ... A stewardess was stabbed. ... They seem to have knives and Mace. ... They said they have a bomb. ... It's getting very bad on the plane. ... Passengers are throwing up and getting sick. ... The plane is making jerky movements. ... I don't think the pilot is flying the plane ... I think we are going down."

**United Flight 175 passenger Peter Hansen's
second cell phone call to his father, Lee Hansen, was recorded.**

Boston Center: As far as the tape, Bobby seemed to think the guy said that "We have planes." I'm gonna reconfirm that for you.

New England Region: Appreciate it.

Unidentified Female Voice: They have what?

Boston Center: Planes, as in plural. There's another one aimed at the World Trade Center.

New England Region: There's another aircraft?

Boston Center: A second one just hit the Trade Center.

New England Region: Okay. Yeah, we gotta alert the military real quick on this.

This conversation between air officials, as transcribed in the 9/11 Commission Report, took place in the time between the crash of American Flight 11 into the North Tower and the crash of United Flight 175 into the South Tower.

Above: *Firefighters, engineers, and FBI agents work at the Pentagon crash site on September 14, 2001.*

Below: *The controls of a commercial airliner such as this 747 are very complex. The hijackers had been attending flight schools within the United States and were prepared to fly the planes.*

they lost track of it on their radar at about 9:34 A.M. Less than four minutes later, a plane crashed into the Pentagon. Within an hour it had been confirmed that the plane that struck the Pentagon was indeed Flight 77.

THE PASSENGERS FIGHT BACK

United Airlines Flight 93 took off late from Newark, New Jersey. It was supposed to take off shortly after 8:00 A.M., but it did not actually leave the ground until 8:42 A.M. By the time Flight 93 was reaching its cruising altitude, air traffic controllers on the ground knew they were facing a major crisis. At 9:24 A.M., Flight 93 received a warning from United Airlines: "Beware any cockpit intrusion—Two a/c [aircrafts] hit World Trade Center." Two minutes later, the Flight 93 pilot asked his controller to confirm the warning. From the plane, air traffic controllers then heard one of the pilots yelling, "Mayday! Get out of here! Get out of here! Get out of here!"

RUSHING THE COCKPIT

As on the first two hijacked planes, passengers and crew members used air phones and cell phones to call people on the ground, reporting that the hijackers were stabbing people and threatening the passengers with a bomb. The people on the ground told them that other planes had been hijacked and had crashed into buildings. Realizing that the terrorists were bluffing about having a bomb the Flight 93 passengers acted quickly. Together, they charged the terrorists. The hijacker pilot, Ziad Jarrah, began flying the plane wildly, trying to stop the passengers from reaching the cockpit. The passengers on Flight 93, however, refused to give up. The plane's flight data recorder captured the sounds of a fierce fight as the passengers struggled with the terrorists to gain entry to the cabin. It also recorded the voices of the terrorists in the cockpit making the decision to crash the plane before the passengers overcame them.

It is not known for certain where the hijackers intended to take Flight 93. The most likely targets were either the White House or the U.S. Capitol, both in Washington, D.C.

TIME LINE
Sept. 11, 2001

8:25 A.M.
Flight 11 hijackers broadcast "We have some planes" message.

8:42 A.M.
United Airlines Flight 93 takes off from Newark International Airport, New Jersey.

8:46 A.M.
Flight 11 crashes into the North Tower of the World Trade Center, New York City. Emergency calls from people in the North Tower reach 9-1-1 operators; FDNY calls in more units to help.

Below: *A fence became a memorial for the victims of United Airlines Flight 93, which crashed in a field in Shanksville, Pennsylvania.*

Above: *The Twin Towers of the World Trade Center were engulfed in smoke before the towers collapsed.*

Below: *Trainer Ed Apple and his rescue dog, Gus, search for survivors in the Pentagon after the attack. Apple and Gus were part of the Tennessee Task Force One Search and Rescue team.*

A ll those aboard the hijacked planes were killed the instant the planes crashed. Eighty-seven passengers and crew members perished on Flight 11; 60 perished on Flight 175; 59 perished on Flight 77; and 40 perished on Flight 93. At the Pentagon, 125 people in the building were killed, and 106 more were seriously hurt.

MORE THAN WE CAN BEAR

When asked to estimate the number of people killed on the day of the attacks, New York Mayor Rudolph Giuliani replied that the number was likely to be "more than we can bear." No one knows for sure how many people died at the moment each of the two planes slammed into the Twin Towers and how many died when the buildings collapsed. In its report issued in 2004, the 9/11 Commission concluded that 2,973 victims died as a result of all four attacks and crashes. It is estimated that about 2,602 of these people died in the Twin Towers.

IN THE NORTH TOWER

Flight 11 hit the North Tower between its 93rd and 99th floors, causing a huge explosion. Not only did the impact and explosion kill everyone in its path, it also trapped people on the floors above the point of impact. No one above where the plane hit the building could get downstairs because the explosion destroyed the stairways. From the time of impact, the damage spread quickly through the building. The explosion caused by the crash sent a fireball of burning jet fuel down at least one elevator shaft, causing explosions and fires on several lower floors.

Emergency calls poured in to the authorities, including the New York Police Department (NYPD), the New York Fire Department (FDNY), and the Port Authority Police Department (PAPD). Because so many people called "9-1-1" the system was overwhelmed. Many callers could not get through. There was no single plan for dealing with the emergency. At times, the authorities from different agencies gave out different information. Fire-safety officials at the scene say

that they began evacuation of the building within minutes of the crash. No one, however, told the emergency operators to advise evacuation, and many told callers from the North Tower to stay where they were and await help. Another problem was that many people did not hear the evacuation call because the crash had knocked out the building's public address system in many places. Not realizing the danger they were in, some people stopped to gather their belongings. A few even tried to keep working. Most people who could get out of the building did just that, in spite of instructions by some 9-1-1 operators to wait for help.

Above: On September 12, 2001, New York Governor George Pataki, New York City Mayor Rudolph Giuliani, and U.S. Senator Hillary Rodham Clinton of New York took a grim tour of Ground Zero—the site where the Twin Towers had stood.

DIFFICULT CHOICES

About ten minutes after the plane hit the building, the rising smoke and heat were making it unbearable for those trapped above the point of impact in the North Tower. The NYPD considered trying a rooftop helicopter rescue, but the fire and smoke made it impossible. Unable to stand the smoke and heat, many people jumped to their deaths from the burning tower. To many observers, the sight of people jumping from the high stories was one of the most horrifying parts of the tragic day.

IN THE SOUTH TOWER

Many people decided to leave the South Tower as soon as they realized that a plane had been flown into the North Tower. As in the North Tower, not everyone in the South Tower got clear instructions from authorities.

TIME LINE
Sept. 11, 2001

ABOUT 8:47 A.M.
NYPD helicopters try rooftop rescue at the North Tower but fail because of flames and smoke.

8:52 A.M.
Firefighters arriving at the North Tower find injured people in the lobby and send scouts to upper floors.

Above: Workers flee the burning Twin Towers.

8:57 A.M.
FDNY chiefs give instructions to evacuate the South Tower.

8:58 A.M.
NYPD orders 1,000 officers to the World Trade Center.

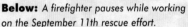

Below: A firefighter pauses while working on the September 11th rescue effort.

"At 9:05 a friend of Mr. Alderman's at Bloomberg sent out an e-mail to him, saying, 'Pete, if you get this please let me know that you're okay.'

At 9:07, Mr. Alderman responded, 'THERE IS A lot of SMOKE.'

Simultaneously he was talking online with his sister, Jane Alderman.

He told her at 9:07, 'I'm SCARED THERE IS A lot OF SMOKE.'

She e-mailed him several more times, ending with this question, 'Can you get out of there?'

Mr. Alderman replied at 9:16 A.M. 'No we are stuck.'"

The New York Times reported on a series of e-mail messages between Peter Alderman, an unidentified friend, and his sister. Peter Alderman was on the 106th floor of the North Tower when it was hit.

@

Some people who were trying to leave the building were advised to go back to their offices. Some who called the police for instructions were advised to leave, while others were told to wait for more instructions. By the time the FDNY ordered the evacuation of the building at 9:02 A.M., it was too late to save everyone. One minute later, Flight 175 crashed into the South Tower between the 77th and 85th floors.

THE SURVIVOR'S STAIRWAY

As in the North Tower, people had trouble getting clear information about what was happening. The luckiest were those a few floors below the point of impact. Most of them found stairways with working lights and no smoke. Because of the angle at which Flight 175 hit the South Tower, one stairway remained usable. A few people above the point of impact who found the open stairway were able to descend safely. For many, however, darkness and increasing smoke led to confusion. Some people above the point of impact actually climbed up the stairs to get away from the fire and smoke.

RESCUE OPERATIONS

Soon after Flight 11 hit the North Tower, firefighters began responding to the emergency. As hundreds of firefighters headed toward the blaze, they quickly realized they would not be able to fight the huge fire. They decided that their main job was rescuing people. As workers and others descended the North Tower stairs, they met firefighters carrying

Above: *Some people watch in stunned disbelief while others flee in terror as a cloud of dust and debris rolls down a street following the collapse of one of the Twin Towers.*

🎞 FILM EXCERPT 📖 GOVERNMENT DOCUMENT 🎤 INTERVIEW/BOOK EXTRACT 🎵 SONG EXCERPT

Above: Members of the New York Fire Department sit in silence following the collapse of one of the Twin Towers. Hundreds of their fellow firefighters were trapped in the World Trade Center.

9:00 A.M.
FDNY chiefs call in additional units to focus on rescue efforts.

9:02 A.M.
Evacuation order is broadcast on the South Tower public address system.

Below: An American flag and wreath rest on one of the fences surrounding Ground Zero.

heavy loads of equipment on their way up. The Port Authority, which operated the World Trade Center, had a command based at the WTC, and PAPD officers from other posts rushed to the scene. New York City's Chief of Police sent almost 1,000 officers to the World Trade Center. As New York City's police and firefighters entered the buildings, they had little information about what they would find as they ascended. When Flight 175 hit the South Tower, both the FDNY and the NYPD called in even more members. Many firefighters whose shifts were ending stayed on duty to join the rescue.

Despite their bravery, New York's police and firefighting forces were not ready for a disaster the size of the September 11th attacks. New York City had an Office of Emergency Management that was supposed to get all of the city's emergency agencies to work together to respond to a major disaster. The NYPD and the FDNY, however, were not set up to work together. Among

Left A police officer helps a woman after the collapse of the Twin Towers.

"He called right after the first plane hit. ... He said, 'I just wanted you to know that a plane hit the other tower. I'm okay—but here we go again.' He had been [there] in 1993 during the first bombing. 'I wanted you to turn on the TV because it's going to be the top story of the day,' he said.
After watching for a minute, I felt that the building was in jeopardy, so I called him back.
'Honey, get out.' He said, 'No, it's okay'—in the background, an announcement started over the PA ... saying that there was no need to evacuate. A moment later, we each got other calls and signed off. Then the second plane struck."

Linda Perry Thorpe spoke to her husband, Eric, who worked in the South Tower, before the building was hit. Eric was on the 87th floor and died in the attack.

Left: *Clouds of dust, smoke, and ash rise from the site where the Twin Towers stood.*

the biggest problems that the emergency responders from different agencies faced was that their radios did not allow them to communicate with each other. Additionally, New York City's emergency command center was located in the World Trade Center and was rendered inoperable. The decision to put the center in this location was made by New York City Mayor Rudy Giuliani, despite warnings by some emergency experts. However, in spite of the problems they faced, New York City's firefighters, police officers, and other emergency responders did their jobs with great heroism, leading many people to safety.

Below: *Firefighters raise the American flag at Ground Zero.*

THE TOWERS FALL

By now, firefighting officials knew that the Twin Towers were severely damaged and that the tops of the buildings might collapse. Just before 10:00 A.M., the South Tower collapsed. With a huge roar, one of New York's two tallest buildings was gone within ten seconds. As the building fell floor by floor, anyone inside was killed. The collapse blew debris far into the surrounding streets, sending people running for their lives. People in the North Tower heard the roar, but many did not know what had caused it. Fire and police officials rushed to order firefighters and police officers out of the North Tower. About five minutes after the South Tower fell,

📽 FILM EXCERPT 📄 GOVERNMENT DOCUMENT 🎙 INTERVIEW/BOOK EXTRACT 🎵 SONG EXCERPT

Above: *The attack on the Pentagon left a large gaping hole in one side of the building.*

TIME LINE
Sept. 11, 2001

9:03 A.M.
Flight 175 crashes into the South Tower of the World Trade Center.

9:15 A.M.
FDNY calls in additional firefighters and rescue teams.

9:19 A.M.
United Airlines warns all its pilots against the threat of possible cockpit intrusions.

police officers in helicopters radioed that the top of the North Tower was glowing red, and said they did not think the building would stand for long. The North Tower collapsed at 10:28 A.M.

INSIDE THE PENTAGON

American Airlines Flight 77 hit the west wall of the Pentagon. Although it is only four stories tall, the Pentagon is the biggest office building in the United States. Inside, the Pentagon has five rings of corridors surrounding a courtyard. Flight 77 nearly crashed through all five rings, but the damage did not spread through the whole building. As in New York City, nearly every available firefighter and police officer reported for duty. While they were pulling survivors out of the Pentagon, reports came of another hijacked plane headed for Washington. This was United Flight 93. Thanks to the bravery of the passengers on Flight 93, many lives on the ground were probably saved.

Left: *Police help a survivor after the attack.*

"I see Officer Smith's face in my mind every day. ... She was scared, her eyes said as much. But most of all she was courageous. ... Heroism is not only running into flames. It is doing your job in the face of horror. ...

'Don't look, keep moving,' she told us; she was shielding you from seeing the destruction. People would have backed up and caused a logjam, she was looking everybody in the eye. No doubt she saw the situation and thought people would stop. She saved hundreds of people.

When I got out of the World Trade Center ... I saw my building collapse. I knew ... Officer Smith was still inside.

I wrote a letter to the [New York Police] Department to make sure they were aware of her heroism. 'There is no doubt,' I wrote, 'that NYPD Officer Smith saved dozens, if not hundreds of lives.'"

Martin Glynn, a computer programmer who worked in the South Tower, remembers Officer Moira Smith, a police officer who saved many lives before being killed in the tower's collapse.

When Flight 11 hit the North Tower, many people thought it was a terrible accident. However, as soon as Flight 175 struck the South Tower and people became aware of the other hijackings, nearly everyone knew the United States had been attacked by terrorists.

Above: On September 12, 2001, newspapers around the world led with headlines of the terrorist attacks.

Below: A U.S. Air Force F-16 fighter flies over New York City on September 24, 2003, as part of a NORAD mission.

UNDER ATTACK

Around the country, people were glued to TV, radio, and Internet news sources. Many worried about relatives and friends in New York City and Washington, and about whether more attacks were on the way. Air travel was shut down completely, and the financial markets closed. Across the United States and around the world, the headlines of September 12 declared that the United States had been attacked.

AIR DEFENSE

About 12 minutes after air traffic controllers in Boston knew that Flight 11 had been hijacked, they alerted officials from NEADS, the Northeast Air Defense Sector. NEADS is part of NORAD, the North American Aerospace Defense Command. NORAD is the federal agency responsible for the defense of U.S. airspace. Less than 10 minutes later, NEADS had scrambled fighter jets from Otis Air Force Base, in Massachusetts, in order to try to intercept the hijacked planes. They were too late. Barely a minute after the fighters took off, Flight 11 hit the North Tower. NEADS did not even know about a second hijacked plane until about the same time Flight 175 hit the South Tower. Other fighter jets were scrambled from Langley Air Force Base, in Virginia, and sent toward Washington, D.C. They did not make it in time to prevent Flight 77 from crashing into the Pentagon. When

FILM EXCERPT 🎞 GOVERNMENT DOCUMENT 📄 INTERVIEW/BOOK EXTRACT 🎤 SONG EXCERPT 🎵

authorities realized they were dealing with multiple hijackings, the Federal Aviation Administration (FAA) grounded all flights across the country. No planes were allowed to take off, and all planes in the air were instructed to land as soon as possible. In a few hours, the FAA grounded about 4,500 planes across the country.

THE PRESIDENT SPEAKS

At the time the attacks occurred, President George W. Bush was visiting an elementary school in Sarasota, Florida. While reading with a class of second-graders in front of an audience of reporters, Bush got the news of airplanes hitting the Twin Towers from an aide. He finished the story and left the classroom for a meeting with his staff. While two hijacked planes were still in the air, Bush held a press conference from the school library. Then, the Secret Service whisked him away, fearing he might be a target for terrorists. Agents flew him first to Barksdale Air Force Base, in Shreveport, Louisiana, and, then to Offut Air Force Base, near Omaha, Nebraska. Once it seemed that the crisis was under control, agents flew the president back to Washington. That night, Bush gave a televised speech declaring that the country would stand up to terrorism.

LEARNING WHAT HAPPENED

In the days after the attacks, the United States struggled to cope with the tragedy. Relatives and friends of people who were in the World Trade Center when it collapsed hung onto fading hopes that their loved ones would be pulled from the wreckage alive, but nearly all were disappointed.

TIME LINE
Sept. 11, 2001

9:37 A.M.
Flight 77 crashes into the Pentagon.

9:58 A.M.
The South Tower of the World Trade Center collapses. FDNY orders firefighters to evacuate North Tower, but some refuse, choosing to stay and help with the rescue effort.

"A great people has been moved to defend a great nation. Terrorist attacks can shake the foundations of our biggest buildings, but they cannot touch the foundation of America. These acts shattered steel, but they cannot dent the steel of American resolve.

America was targeted for attack because we're the brightest beacon for freedom and opportunity in the world. And no one will keep that light from shining.

Today, our nation saw evil, the very worst of human nature. And we responded with the best of America—with the daring of our rescue workers, with the caring for strangers and neighbors who came to give blood and help in any way they could."

Excerpt from President Bush's speech on the night of September 11, 2001.

Left: *President George W. Bush gave a televised speech from the Oval Office in the White House on the night of September 11, 2001.*

Above: *Firefighters and rescue workers remove rubble from the site of the collapsed Twin Towers.*

People quickly learned what took place on the hijacked planes. After flight attendants reported the terrorists' seat numbers, authorities learned their names. Along with the names and faces of the terrorists, another name and face quickly appeared in the news: Osama bin Laden. Osama bin Laden is the leader of al-Qaeda, a group with a goal of establishing an extremely conservative, fundamentalist brand of Islam as the basis for a world order. Al-Qaeda had previously attacked Americans and U.S. targets overseas, and bin Laden and al-Qaeda became the prime suspects for the September 11th attacks. Two of the hijackers, Khalid al-Midhar and Nawaf al-Hazmi, were found to be members of al-Qaeda. Because of a routine airport mix-up, the luggage of another hijacker, Mohamed Atta, did not make it onto his plane. When authorities opened it following the attacks, they found evidence connecting the hijackings to Islamic extremism.

> "Americans have many questions tonight. Americans are asking, 'Who attacked our country?'
>
> The evidence we have gathered all points to a collection of loosely affiliated terrorist organizations known as al-Qaeda. They are some of the murderers indicted for bombing American embassies in Tanzania and Kenya and responsible for bombing the USS *Cole*. ...
>
> Our war on terror begins with al–Qaeda, but it does not end there.
>
> It will not end until every terrorist group of global reach has been found, stopped and defeated. "

Excerpts from President Bush's "War on Terror" speech of September 20, 2001.

THE DEPARTMENT OF HOMELAND SECURITY

On September 20, President Bush gave a speech before both houses of the U.S. Congress. He spoke of how the September 11 attacks affected the American people, and he declared a "war on terror." He also discussed how the country would respond to future terrorists and their supporters, and how the government would change to help keep Americans safe. He announced the creation of the Department of Homeland Security. The leader of the new department— former Pennsylvania governor Tom Ridge—would be a member of the president's cabinet. The job of the new department was to organize all of the parts of the government needed to keep the country safe. Its tasks included securing the country's borders, identifying places that are vulnerable to terrorism, responding to emergencies, regulating immigration, and training law enforcement officers.

THE PATRIOT ACT

Another major aspect of the U.S. government's response to the attacks was a new law, the USA Patriot Act, passed on October 26, 2001. The Patriot Act gave law enforcement agencies greater powers to watch people suspected of terrorism, search for evidence of crimes, detain suspects who

Above: *Search-and-rescue teams used dogs to help search for survivors in the wreckage of the Twin Towers.*

TIME LINE
Sept. 11, 2001

10:04 A.M.
NYPD helicopter operator warns that the North Tower roof is glowing red and the top 15 floors look ready to collapse.

10:08 A.M.
Another NYPD helicopter pilot warns that the North Tower looks unstable.

10:24 A.M.
About five FDNY companies return to the North Tower lobby but do not immediately evacuate.

10:28 A.M.
The North Tower of the World Trade Center collapses.

were not U.S. citizens, and share information. Some Americans worried that the Patriot Act would reduce people's civil liberties by allowing the government to spy on them. In spite of these worries, the government renewed the Patriot Act in March 2006.

BIOTERRORISM

New fears were spawned by different types of terrorism scares. In late 2001, concentrated anthrax spores mailed in letters killed five people, raising the fear of bioterrorism. Anthrax is a disease that can be transmitted when

Above: *Tom Ridge, then leader of the U.S. Department of Homeland Security, gives a speech in Washington, D.C., on January 24, 2003.*

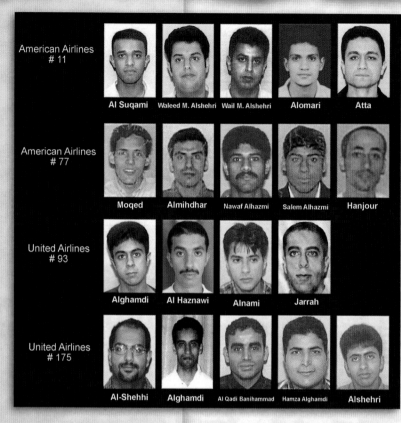

American Airlines # 11	Al Suqami	Waleed M. Alshehri	Wail M. Alshehri	Alomari	Atta
American Airlines # 77	Moqed	Almihdhar	Nawaf Alhazmi	Salem Alhazmi	Hanjour
United Airlines # 93	Alghamdi	Al Haznawi	Alnami	Jarrah	
United Airlines # 175	Al-Shehhi	Alghamdi	Al Qadi Banihammad	Hamza Alghamdi	Alshehri

Above: On September 27, 2001, the U.S. Department of Justice released pictures of the 19 hijackers who carried out the 9/11 terrorist attacks.

spores are ingested, inhaled, or put in contact with open wounds on the skin. In December 2001, passengers on an American Airlines flight from Paris to Miami stopped Richard Reid from lighting the fuse of a bomb hidden in his shoes. On May 8 2002, Jose Padilla was arrested. Padilla, a U.S. citizen, was suspected of plotting to set off a radioactive "dirty bomb" in the United States. A dirty bomb combines radioactive material with explosives. It causes radioactive contamination to all those in the nearby area. Although he was not convicted of this charge, he was sentenced to more than 17 years in prison for plotting to kill Americans overseas and for supporting and helping to finance terrorist organizations. Padilla also allegedly met with members of al-Qaeda.

SEPTEMBER 11 AND IRAQ

The fear of terrorism has also affected U.S. foreign policy, in part as a result of the Bush administration's declared "war on terror." The United States

"The act did four things. It tore down the bureaucratic wall that had been imposed between law enforcement and intelligence, allowing cooperation and information sharing. That's been very valuable.

The Patriot Act, secondly, strengthened criminal laws against terrorism.

Third, it helped speed the investigation of terrorist threats, putting agents on the street instead of behind desks doing paperwork to pursue terrorists untrapped in their offices.

And finally, the Patriot Act updated our anti-terrorism laws to reflect new technologies and to give us the same tools used to fight against drug dealers and organized crime so that we can fight against terrorists."

Attorney General John Ashcroft commented on the Patriot Act, June 8, 2004.

Right: Former U.S. Secretary of State Colin Powell and other members of the Bush administration argued that Saddam Hussein's Iraq harbored weapons of mass destruction that could be used against the United States.

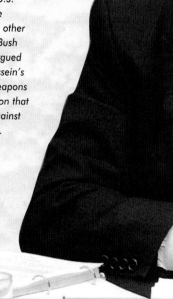

Above: A worker reads a newspaper as he waits outside the offices of New York Governor George Pataki after tests found signs of anthrax in the building.

TIME LINE
Sept. 11, 2001

SEPTEMBER 13, 2001
Air travel resumes in the United States.

SEPTEMBER 14, 2001
Congress authorizes President Bush to use force against al-Qaeda and Afghanistan.

SEPTEMBER 17, 2001
U.S. financial markets reopen.

SEPTEMBER 20, 2001
President Bush gives a speech announcing the new Department of Homeland Security.

had long been in conflict with Sadam Hussein's Iraq. U.S. government leaders believed Iraq possessed weapons of mass destruction. Some leaders expressed fear that these weapons could fall into the hands of terrorists. This fear played a large role in the invasion of Iraq—the start of a war that created tensions between the United States and many of its allies, as well as caused debate at home.

"I have concluded that this bill still does not strike the right balance between empowering law enforcement and protecting civil liberties. Congress will fulfill its duty only when it protects both the American people and the freedoms at the foundation of American society. So let us preserve our heritage of basic rights. Let us practice as well as preach that liberty. And let us fight to maintain that freedom that we call America."

U.S. Senator Russell Feingold (D-Wisconsin) explained his intention to cast the only vote against the anti-terrorism bill known as the USA Patriot Act, October 25, 2001. He did so on the grounds that it violates civil liberties guaranteed by the U.S. Constitution.

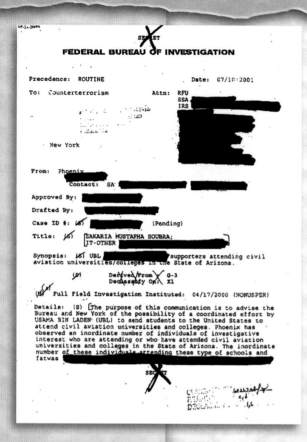

Above: The "Phoenix Memo" shows that the FBI suspected al-Qaeda might use airplanes in a terrorist attack.

Osama bin Laden and al-Qaeda were not known to most Americans until after September 11, 2001. But they were known by U.S. government leaders and members of the intelligence community. In July 2001, FBI agents in Phoenix, Arizona, sent a memo warning of bin Laden supporters taking flying classes in Arizona. A little more than one month before the attacks, the Presidential Daily Brief included the warning "bin Laden Determined to Strike in U.S."

AL-QAEDA HISTORY

Al-Qaeda got its start in Afghanistan in the late 1980s. From 1979 to 1988, the Soviet Union had invaded Afghanistan and was attempting to set up a pro-Soviet government. The battle in Afghanistan drew thousands of Islamist fighters, called "mujahideen," from around the world to fight a "jihad," or struggle, against the Soviet giant. It was the time of the Cold War, a period of intense rivalry between the United States and the Soviet Union. The United States gave millions of dollars and weapons to help fight Soviet expansion. One of the Islamists who went to fight in Afghanistan was Osama bin Laden. A son of one of the wealthiest families in Saudi Arabia, bin Laden became an important figure in the struggle against the Soviet Union by giving money to the cause. He also helped create an organization that brought Islamist fighters to Afghanistan. By the time the Soviet Union pulled out of Afghanistan, bin Laden had made his name as the leader of an Islamist group called al-Qaeda, or "the Base." He had also made contacts with other Islamist leaders, including Ayman al-Zawahiri, who was a major figure in a group called Egyptian Islamic Jihad.

Left: Osama bin Laden sits in a cave in Afghanistan (1988).

Above: *Mujahideen fighters in Afghanistan battled the Soviet Union in the 1980s.*

SEPTEMBER–NOVEMBER 2001
Letters containing deadly anthrax spores are mailed to news media offices and to two Democratic U.S. senators, killing five people and infecting 17 others.

OCTOBER 7, 2001
Operation Enduring Freedom, the invasion designed to find Osama bin Laden and eradicate al-Qaeda, begins. The United States launches air strikes and raids in Afghanistan.

THE GULF WAR

Bin Laden moved back to Saudi Arabia in 1990. Later that year, Saudi Arabia's neighbor Iraq invaded the small, oil–rich nation of Kuwait. Bin Laden suggested the Saudi government use al-Qaeda to fight Iraq, but the Saudis turned him down. The Saudi government instead allowed the United States and other Western nations to base their forces in Saudi Arabia while fighting Iraq. This enraged bin Laden. He became an enemy of his own country and was exiled to Sudan. Bin Laden began moving al-Qaeda to Sudan, where an Islamic government was growing in power.

Above: *A tank rides through the streets of Kabul, Afghanistan, during the Soviet invasion.*

"As more recruits were trained in Afghanistan during the late 1990s, so ever more terrorist attacks were prepared. In the aftermath of the 1998 U.S. embassy bombings, men controlled or encouraged by Osama bin Laden were responsible for planning an array of horrendous atrocities. Cells plotted to kill President Bush, destroy … U.S. embassies in New Delhi, Paris, and Albania, and launch a multi-continent attack."

Simon Reeve was the first author to write a book about Osama bin Laden and al-Qaeda, The New Jackals. First published in 1998, it was updated after the events of 9/11.

Above: *A Norwegian commercial lift ship brings the USS Cole back to the United States for repairs after it was attacked by al-Qaeda.*

GROWING IN STRENGTH

While in Sudan, bin Laden built al-Qaeda into a powerful and dangerous group. Its goal was promote Islamic government and to fight anyone who stood in its way. His main enemy became the United States.

THE TALIBAN

By 1996, Sudan's government had turned against bin Laden. However, the new Islamic government of Afghanistan, a group called the Taliban, welcomed him and al-Qaeda. The Taliban started out as a movement of students, but by 1996 they had turned Afghanistan into a dictatorship governed by their very strict version of Islam. Bin Laden built al-Qaeda training camps in Afghanistan and used that nation as a base for numerous terrorist plots.

Below: *Zacarias Moussaoui was arrested in the United States for having an expired visa after his flight instructor reported him to the FBI as a possible terrorist.*

ATTACKS ON U.S. EMBASSIES

In February 1998, bin Laden issued a religious order called a *fatwa* that declared Muslims had a duty to kill Americans. Six months later on August 7, 1998, al-Qaeda members drove trucks loaded with bombs into the U.S. embassies in two African cities—Nairobi, Kenya, and Dar es Salaam, Tanzania. In Nairobi, 213 people were killed, including 12 Americans, and about 5,000 were injured. In Dar es Salaam, 11 people were killed. Al-Qaeda faxed messages to London taking responsibility for the attacks. The United States responded, a few

Right: *Ayman al-Zawahiri has been al-Qaeda's second-in-command leader.*

weeks later, by shooting missiles at an al-Qaeda training camp in Afghanistan and a chemical-weapons plant in Sudan, but this failed to kill bin Laden. In October 2000, al-Qaeda struck again. Using a small boat filled with explosives, al-Qaeda suicide bombers blew a hole in the side of the USS *Cole*, killing 17 and injuring 47.

RUNNING OUT OF TIME

U.S. government officials knew that al-Qaeda was a threat to Americans. U.S. intelligence agencies heard from sources that a major attack was planned, but they did not know details. A few months after the USS *Cole* attack in 2000, all of the al-Qaeda terrorists who would pilot planes on 9/11 were already in the United States taking flying lessons. During late 2000 and early 2001, the remaining hijackers got visas to enter the United States and went to al-Qaeda training camps in Afghanistan. By July 2001, they were all in the United States.

MISSED OPPORTUNITIES

Most of the terrorists were not known to U.S. law enforcement and intelligence agencies. While preparing for the attacks, the terorists tried not to draw attention to themselves. Two of the terrorists, however, were known members of al-Qaeda. The Federal Bureau of Investigation (FBI) and the Central Intelligence Agency (CIA) believed that Khalid al-Midhar and Nawaf al-Hazmi were involved in the *Cole* bombing. Even though some agents were very worried by having terrorists loose in the United States, the FBI and the CIA could not agree on how to handle the case of al-Midhar and al-Hazmi and did not take action to find them. In another case, a flight instructor suspected a student, Zacarias Moussaoui, might be a terrorist and reported him to the FBI. Finding that Moussaoui was in the United States illegally, the FBI

TIME LINE
2001

OCTOBER 26, 2001
Congress passes the USA Patriot Act.

DECEMBER 18, 2001
Congress passes resolution declaring September 11th Patriot Day.

DECEMBER 22, 2001
American Airlines passengers foil British-born "shoebomber" Richard Reid.

August 2001: The FBI does not recognize the significance of information regarding al-Mihdhar and al-Hazmi's possible arrival in the United States. The FBI does not give priority to the search.

August 2001: FBI headquarters does not recognize the significance of the information regarding Moussaoui's training and beliefs and thus does not give sufficient priority to determining what Moussaoui might be planning.

August 2001: The CIA and FBI do not connect the presence of al-Mihdhar, al-Hazmi, and Moussaoui to the general threat reporting about imminent attacks.

Missed opportunities by the CIA to use and communicate information gathered on the hijackers in the United States during the months before the attacks were documented in the 9/11 Commission report.

Above: *Firefighters respond to the al-Qaeda bombing of the U.S. embassy in Nairobi, Kenya.*

Above: *U.S. Special Forces soldiers pose for a picture with members of the Northern Alliance, allies in the fight against the Taliban. The American soldiers' faces have been blurred to protect their identities.*

arrested him in August 2001 but did not search his belongings. It was not until after the attacks that they discovered he was connected to al-Qaeda. No one knows whether better intelligence work could have stopped the attacks. It is possible, however, that connecting al-Qaeda members in the United States to the idea of using airplanes as bombs could have saved thousands of lives.

AFTER THE ATTACKS

After the 9/11 attacks, the U.S. government was jolted into action. Other nations such as Britain, Spain, and Australia rushed to support the United States. President Bush demanded that the Taliban turn over bin Laden and other al-Qaeda leaders. When the Taliban refused, the United States put together a coalition of allies and invaded Afghanistan. The coalition found support even in Afghanistan. The Northern Alliance, an Afghan rebel group that opposed the Taliban, worked with the international coalition.

The coalition quickly toppled the Taliban from power. Finding bin Laden and other al-Qaeda leaders proved harder. In one battle known as Tora Bora, coalition forces thought they had a chance of catching bin Laden, but he got away. After the battle, the U.S. military was criticized for giving too much reponsibility in the fight to the Northern Alliance rather than using its own highly trained soldiers.

"We calculated in advance the number of casualties from the enemy, who would be killed based on the position of the tower. We calculated that the floors that would be hit would be three or four floors. I was the most optimistic of them all ... due to my experience in this field, I was thinking that the fire from the gas in the plane would melt the iron structure of the building and collapse the area where the plane hit and all the floors above it only. This is all that we had hoped for."

Osama bin Laden discusses the 9/11 attacks in this transcript excerpt from a video broadcast in the United States on December 13, 2001.

⊙ **FILM EXCERPT** ▣ **GOVERNMENT DOCUMENT** ⭘ **INTERVIEW/BOOK EXTRACT** ♪ **SONG EXCERPT**

Above: U.S. newspaper headlines following the July 7, 2005, bombings in London shocked readers. Four Islamist suicide bombers detonated bombs on underground trains and buses, killing 56 people and injuring hundreds. One of the bombers recorded a video statement in which he warned of further attacks if British troops were not immediately pulled out of Iraq and Afghanistan.

AL-QAEDA TODAY

Although the United States supported a new democratically elected government in Afghanistan, the country continued to struggle. In mid 2008, there were reports that the Taliban was regaining strength. In the years following the 9/11 attacks, al-Qaeda continued to carry out terrorist attacks—including the July 7 attacks and the March 11, 2004 attacks in Madrid, Spain, where four commuter trains were ripped apart by bombs, killing 192 people and injuring hundreds. Meanwhile, bin Laden remained at large.

Left: A U.S. Special Forces soldier stands guard for a U.S. official visiting Afghanistan in November 2001.

Above: *Patriotic bumper stickers became common after the 9/11 attacks.*

In movies, music, television, and visual art, many creative people have explored the meaning of the 9/11 attacks, and the effects of the attacks on individuals and on the nation. People have worn their feelings on everything from T-shirts to car bumper stickers.

RESPONSE FROM ENTERTAINERS

Many artists, musicians, and entertainers used their talents to raise money for relief efforts after the attacks. Less than two weeks after September 11, music stars Alicia Keys, Tom Petty, Willie Nelson, U2, Sting, Stevie Wonder, Bruce Springsteen, and the Dixie Chicks performed in a telethon. Broadcast on four major TV networks with no commercials, *America: A Tribute to Heroes* raised more than $150 million for the families of the victims of the attacks. The following month, the "Concert for New York City" featured more stars, including Mick Jagger and Keith Richards of the Rolling Stones, Sir Paul McCartney, Elton John, Billy Joel, Jay-Z, and The Who. Famous comedians including Billy Crystal and Adam Sandler also took part. The concert was held in New York City's Madison Square Garden. Most of the audience was made up of New York City police officers and firefighters and their families. The concert honored victims of the attacks, as well as those who worked to find and rescue survivors. It raised more than $35 million for victims' families.

One of the last performances of the "Concert for New York City" was former Beatle

"I know I said I love you
I know you know it's true
I've got to put the phone down
And do what we gotta do
One's standing in the aisleway
Two more at the door
We've got to get inside there
Before they kill some more

Time is running out
Let's roll
Time is running out
Let's roll"

Lyrics from Neil Young's **Let's Roll.** *The title of the song is taken from a phrase used by Todd Beamer, a passenger on Flight 93, before he helped storm the cockpit.*

🎵

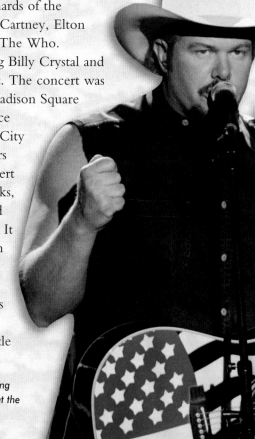

Right: *Toby Keith performs his hit song* Courtesy of the Red, White, and Blue *at the Country Music Awards in May 2002.*

Above: *Destiny's Child performs at the Concert for New York City on October 20, 2001.*

MARCH 2002
Jules and Gedeon Naudet's *9/11* is shown on TV.

MARCH 11, 2002
Tribute in Light first appears six months after the attacks.

JULY 4, 2002
Toby Keith's *Courtesy of the Red, White, and Blue (The Angry American)* is #1 on Billboard's country singles chart.

AUGUST 17, 2002
Bruce Springsteen's *The Rising* goes to #1 on the Billboard 200 chart.

Sir Paul McCartney singing *Freedom*, written shortly after the attacks. Another famous song inspired by the attacks of 9/11 is Neil Young's *Let's Roll*. Many other popular recording artists have written songs inspired by 9/11. Bruce Springsteen's 2002 album, *The Rising*, reflected the singer's thoughts about the attacks. Country singer Toby Keith had a hit with *Courtesy of the Red, White, and Blue (The Angry American)*, a song about fighting back against attacks on the United States. Rapper and movie star Will Smith's 2005 song *Tell Me Why* reflected on watching TV coverage of September 11 with his children.

In classical music, contemporary composer John Coolidge Adams wrote *On the Transmigration of Souls*, a 30-minute piece that combined recorded sounds of New York City, voices reading the names of the September 11 victims, along with an orchestra and chorus. The piece was first performed by the New York Philharmonic in 2002. In 2003, it won the Pulitzer Prize in music.

"After September 11th I suddenly found answers to so many questions. I sometimes questioned if I was wasting my life being a musician, and was searching for a purpose to continue. Then I realized how important it is—when the world becomes ugly, it takes each of us to balance the world in the direction of beauty. That's the musician's role in this world—to make the world a better place, and outweigh the ugliness of the world, by filling the world with beauty. I have a chance to help people with my music. So I'm donating all the money I receive for the 9.11 CD to the Red Cross."

Ron "Bumblefoot" Thal, an independent recording artist, titled one of his CDs 9.11.

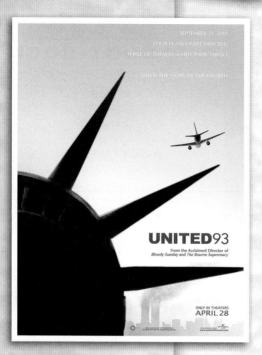

Above: *This poster advertises the movie* United 93, *a re-enactment of the events over Pennsylvania. It was released in 2006.*

"New York City has traditionally served as the backdrop for many comic books that have entertained readers for decades. ... I think we all now realize that we do not have to read fiction to find examples of heroism. The real heroes in American life have been with us all along. Our firefighters, police officers, and other rescue workers put their lives on the line every day to protect the rest of us from danger."

Former New York City Mayor Rudolph Giuliani wrote the foreword to Marvel Comics' A Moment of Silence *special edition.*

LITERATURE AND COMICS

Hundreds of books have been published about September 11. Nonfiction books have looked at everything from the events leading up to the attacks, to government responses, to the stories of survivors and witnesses. Famous fiction writers, including John Updike, Jonathan Safran Foer, and Martin Amis, have also set stories in the days after the attacks.

A special issue in the *Amazing Spider-Man* series paid tribute to the firefighters and rescue workers of 9/11. Some comic book companies such as Marvel produced special editions and donated the profits to charity.

MOVIES

In 2001, French filmmakers Jules and Gedeon Naudet were working on a documentary about New York City firefighters. While riding with the firefighters on the morning of September 11, Jules heard a low-flying plane and began filming it just before it hit the North Tower. As the firefighters responded to the attacks on the World Trade Center, he kept filming. The Naudets' film

Right: *Scene from a special edition comic called* Heroes *which honors the firemen who saved lives on 9/11.*

turned into a documentary about New York firefighters on the day of the attacks. Titled *9/11*, it was shown on TV in March 2002. Also in 2002, French producer Alain Brigand came out with *September 11th*. For this film, Brigand commissioned 11 filmmakers from around the world to make short movies—each 11 minutes, 9 seconds, and 1 frame long—that express views of the attacks.

About five years after the attacks, Hollywood began releasing movies about September 11. *United 93* (2006) and *Flight 93* (2006) explored the drama of the plane that crashed in a Pennsylvania field when the passengers fought the terrorists. *World Trade Center* (2006) starred Nicolas Cage as real-life Port Authority police sergeant John McLoughlin who survived the

Left: World Trade Center *star Nicolas Cage holds a press conference on September 12, 2006, to discuss the opening of his movie based on the attack on the Twin Towers.*

SEPTEMBER 11, 2002
Tribute in Light marks the first anniversary of the attacks.

JANUARY 2004
The design for the National September 11 Memorial & Museum at the World Trade Center is chosen.

MAY 2006
Construction of the National September 11 Memorial & Museum at the World Trade Center begins.

collapse of the South Tower. Other movies used fictional characters to explore the effects of the attacks on individuals. *Reign Over Me* (2007) starred Adam Sandler as a man devastated by the loss of his family in one of the hijacked planes. *The Great New Wonderful* (2005) looked at the effect of the attacks on New Yorkers one year later. In the movie, the characters struggle with the memory of the tragedy without ever mentioning it.

FINE ARTS

On September 11, the collapse of the Twin Towers destroyed a 70-year-old tree that grew nearby. Even as it was broken, the tree shielded St. Paul's Chapel, one of the oldest buildings in the city, from harm. Sculptor Steve Tobin created a bronze recreation of the tree, called *Trinity Root*, that was installed at the corner of Wall Street and Broadway, near Ground Zero, on September 11, 2005. In 2002, the Metropolitan Museum of New York held an exhibit of photography called "Life of the City" that concluded with monitors showing a constantly changing stream of pictures showing the events of September 11.

"It was a priority for us to show the families of the firemen the truth at the World Trade Center. We finally got all the names together and contacted the families and then sent them a tape. ... I believe it made those families feel a bit better."

Filmmaker Gedeon Naudet talked about showing 9/11 to the families of NYC firefighters who were killed on September 11 2001.

Right: *Trinity Root is a sculpture that encases the roots of the tree that protected St. Paul's Chapel and Trinity Church on 9/11.*

"Timeless in simplicity and beauty, like its landscape, both stark and serene, the Memorial should be quiet in reverence, yet powerful in form, a place both solemn and uplifting.

It should instill pride, and humility. The Memorial should offer intimate experience, yet be heroic in scale. Its strong framework should be open to natural change and allow freedom of personal interpretation.

In this place, a scrap yard will become a gateway and a strip mine will grow into a flowering meadow

But more than restoring health, the Memorial should be radiant, in loving memory of the passengers and crew who gave their lives on Flight 93."

**A statment written by
Paul and Milena Murdoch,
Flight 93 National Memorial architects.**

A fter the 9/11 attacks, Americans showed both their sorrow and their patriotism. Many people displayed American flags on their houses, wore memorial ribbons, and put American flags and memorial bumper stickers on their cars. The attacks came to be known simply as 9/11 and the site where the Twin Towers once stood became known as Ground Zero. All that was left where the Twin Towers stood was a deep crater.

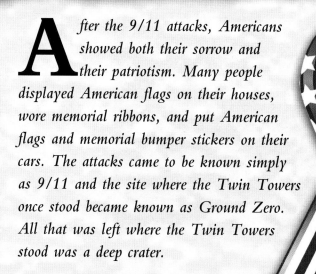

Above:
Many people have worn Stars-and-Stripes ribbons to signify patriotism and remembrance of the victims of the attacks of 9/11.

MEMORIALS

After the attacks, people began using the fence around St. Paul's Chapel, which stands near Ground Zero, as a memorial wall. Family members and friends of those who died in the attacks posted pictures and tributes to their loved ones. Many people—New Yorkers and those visiting the city—spent time at the fence reading the tributes. Six months after the attacks, New York City remembered the Twin Towers by shining 88 powerful beams of light upward from Ground Zero. The display was called *Tribute in Light*. It appeared again on September 11, 2002, and it has also appeared every September 11th since then. In early January 2004, a design by architects Michael Arad and Peter Walker won a competition for the National September 11 Memorial & Museum at the World Trade Center. The memorial will take up eight acres (32,000 square meters), and it will include pools of water into which will flow the largest humanmade waterfalls in the United States. Construction began in May 2006. The memorial is projected to open in 2011.

Below: Tribute in Light, *in which twin beams of light take the place of the Twin Towers, shines up from Ground Zero.*

Right: A memorial in New York City for loved ones who died in the Twin Towers.

JUNE 2005
Freedom Tower design is released.

SEPTEMBER 7, 2005
Flight 93 Memorial plan is announced.

SEPTEMBER 11 2008
The memorial park at the Pentagon opens.

2011
National September 11 Memorial & Museum at the World Trade Center planned to open in time for tenth anniversary of attacks.

At the Pentagon, a memorial park opened in September 2008 features 184 individual memorial units—125 representing people killed in the Pentagon and 59 for those killed aboard Flight 77. The National Parks Service runs Flight 93 National Memorial, located in Pennsylvania. The memorial features 40 large wind chimes and 40 memorial maple groves—one for each victim—as well as ponds and a Field of Honor that marks the crash site.

YEARLY REMEMBRANCE

On December 18, 2001, the United States Congress passed a resolution saying that each September 11 in the future would be observed as Patriot Day. On the anniversary of the attacks, President Bush met at Ground Zero with families that lost members in the attacks. People in New York held candlelight vigils around the city. New York City mayor Michael Bloomberg dedicated an eternal memorial light in Battery Park to the victims of the attacks.

"On Patriot Day, we remember the innocent victims, and we pay tribute to the valiant firefighters, police officers, emergency personnel, and ordinary citizens who risked their lives. ...

The spirit of our people is the source of America's strength, and six years ago, Americans came to the aid of neighbors in need. On Patriot Day, we pray for those who died and for their families."

President George W. Bush made a proclamation on Patriot Day, 2007.

Left: Visitors to Ground Zero gather to read through the tributes and information at the site.

SEPTEMBER II

Above: *An artist's conception shows what the New York City skyline will look like after Freedom Tower is completed.*

Above: *A memorial service for the victims of the 9/11 terrorist attacks is held at Ground Zero.*

STILL STRUGGLING

Recovery from the attacks and remembrance of those lost have become a part of American life. In spite of all the response, recovery, and memorial efforts, however, some studies have shown that many survivors of the attacks are still deeply traumatized. Organizations such as the World Trade Center Survivors Network help survivors cope with the aftermath of the attacks by providing peer support and counseling services. The group has also worked to help preserve the Survivor's Stairway. Many survivors of the attacks escaped the North Tower by this stairway, and it was the last piece of the Twin Towers left standing in its original place. The Survivor's Stairway was relocated to the National September 11 Memorial & Museum at the World Trade Center.

SEPTEMBER 11 AND U.S. POLITICS

The attacks of 9/11 have affected politics in the United States, as has the war in Iraq that was launched in part on the belief that Iraq was harboring weapons of mass destruction that might be used in a terrorist attacks. In the 2004 election, incumbent Republican candidate George W. Bush and Democratic challenger John Kerry presented different ideas about how to best keep Americans safe

"I was driving to a state legislative hearing in downtown Chicago when I heard the news on my car radio: a plane had hit the World Trade Center. By the time I got to my meeting, the second plane had hit, and we were told to evacuate.

People gathered in the streets and looked up at the sky and the Sears Tower, transformed from a workplace to a target. We feared for our families and our country. We mourned the terrible loss suffered by our fellow citizens. Back at my law office, I watched the images from New York: a plane vanishing into glass and steel; men and women clinging to windowsills, then letting go; tall towers crumbling to dust. What we saw that morning forced us to recognize that in a new world of threats, we are no longer protected by our own power. And what we saw that morning was a challenge to a new generation."

President Barack Obama, then a senator, made a speech on August 1, 2007.

from terrorism and how to prevent attacks. In the 2008 presidential election, the ways the United States should deal with the threat of terrorism was again a major topic of debate between Republican candidate John McCain and eventual President Barack Obama, the Democratic candidate.

FREEDOM TOWER

After 9/11, many people wondered whether the Twin Towers would ever be rebuilt. Some thought it was too dangerous. Others thought that not to rebuild would send the message to the terrorists that terrorism had won. By 2003, plans were in place to build a new group of buildings on the World Trade Center site. The centerpiece is the 1,776-foot (541-m) Freedom Tower. Construction on Freedom Tower began in 2006. It is due to be finished in 2012. By mid-2008, people at street level could see the steel supports for the new building begin reaching above the lip of the crater. All those who died in the Twin Towers will always be remembered in Freedom Tower. On some of the steel supports close to the building's foundation, family members of many of the people who perished on September 11, 2001 have written messages to their loved ones.

Above: This aerial view of the future World Trade Center Memorial and Museum is an artist's creation.

Left: Family members of victims write messages on a steel beam forming part of the base of Freedom Tower.

The 9/11 terrorist attacks were shaped and carried out by a number of forceful major figures. The response to the attacks, in turn, was driven by government leaders facing the worst attack on American soil in history. The story of 9/11 is not yet over.

GEORGE W. BUSH (1946–)

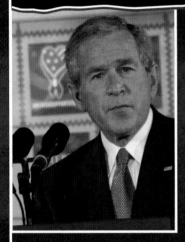

George W. Bush became the 43rd U.S. president in 2001. He is the son of George H. W. Bush, the 41st president, who served from 1989 to 1993. Before he was elected, George W. Bush was governor of Texas. Bush is a member of the Republican Party. In the days after September 11, many Americans viewed him favorably. Bush launched the controversial war in Iraq in 2003, and was reelected in 2004. The war has proved much more difficult to win than his administration initially claimed. No weapons of mass destruction were found to be in existence, and Bush lost support from many Americans. The Republican party lost the election in 2008.

RICHARD CHENEY (1941–)

Dick Cheney, a Wyoming Republican, became U.S. vice president in 2001. Cheney already had a long career in U.S. politics. From the late 1960s through the mid 1970s, he worked for presidents Richard Nixon and Gerald Ford. Returning to Wyoming in the mid–1970s, Cheney won a seat in the House of Representatives and was reelected five times. From 1989 to 1992, he was Secretary of Defense under President George H. W. Bush. From 1992 to 2001, Cheney was chief executive (CEO) of Halliburton, an oil-drilling company based in Texas.

George Tenet (1953–)

President Bill Clinton appointed George Tenet director of the Central Intelligence Agency (CIA) in 1997. Tenet was CIA director from 1997 to 2004. After the attacks of September 11, he faced criticism that the CIA had not done enough to fight al-Qaeda before it struck. He has also been criticized for being too sure that Iraq had weapons of mass destruction. Tenet left the CIA in 2004.

Richard Clarke (1951–)

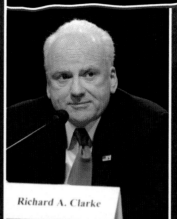

Richard A. Clarke

Richard Clarke began working for the U.S. government in 1973, and was appointed chief counter-terrorism adviser of the National Security Council in 1998. Clarke was aware of the growing threat of attacks by al-Qaeda and pressed the government to increase its opposition. After his retirement in 2003, Clarke's book, *Against All Enemies* (2004), criticized the Bush administration's responsiveness toward the threat of terrorism.

John Ashcroft (1942–)

John Ashcroft was governor of Missouri from 1984 to 1993. In 2000, George W. Bush nominated Ashcroft for U.S. attorney general. As attorney general, Ashcroft promoted the USA Patriot Act, making it easier for government agencies to gather and share information. Ashcroft's critics claimed he had little respect for civil liberties. Ashcroft resigned in 2005.

Rudolph Giuliani (1944–)

Rudy Giuliani was mayor of New York City from 1994 to 2001. He gained national respect for his handling of the 9/11 attacks in the last months of his term. In late 2007, he began seeking the Republican nomination for president, promising to continue the fight against terrorism. By late January 2008, lack of support from voters led him to drop out.

Ramzi Binalshibh (1972-)

Ramzi Binalshibh was originally supposed to be one of the al-Qaeda terrorist pilots in the attacks of September 11, 2001. He was a roommate of Mohamed Atta in Hamburg, Germany. After he was repeatedly denied entry into the United States because of concerns over the possibility that he might become involved in terrorist activities, Binalshibh continued working on the planning and financing of the attacks. He was arrested after a gunfight in Karachi, Pakistan, on September 11, 2002. Binalshibh is also believed to have been involved with the al-Qaeda attack on the USS *Cole* in 2000. As of 2008, he was in prison at the U.S. military base in Guantanamo Bay, Cuba.

Osama bin Laden (1957–)

Osama bin Laden comes from one of Saudi Arabia's richest families. Around 1980, he went to Afghanistan to fight the Soviet Union. He used his wealth to fund recruitment and training of fighters and met Ayman al-Zawahiri. The two joined their groups into al-Qaeda, a larger militant Islamist group. Bin Laden is hostile toward the United States. Al-Qaeda has organized many acts of terrorism, including the 9/11 attacks. Since the invasion of Afghanistan following September 11, 2001, bin Laden has been one of the most wanted men in the world. Many believe he is hiding in the mountains between Afghanistan and Pakistan; some think he may already be dead.

Ayman al-Zawahiri (1951–)

Ayman al-Zawahiri was born in Egypt and educated as a doctor. He joined the Muslim Brotherhood as a teenager and went on to become a major leader of Egyptian Islamic Jihad. In the 1980s, Zawahiri was arrested and jailed in connection with the assassination of Egyptian president Anwar al-Sadat. By the late 1980s, he had joined forces with bin Laden and also become bin Laden's personal physician. He is said to be al-Qaeda's second-in-command and one of the group's top strategists. Along with bin Laden, Zawahiri is one of the world's most wanted terrorists. In 2006, the United States fired a missile at a target in Pakistan in a failed attempt to kill Zawahiri.

Mohammed Omar (1959–)

Mullah Mohammed Omar is the leader of the Taliban, the Islamist group that ruled Afghanistan from 1996 to late 2001. Omar fought the Soviet Union when it tried to take over Afghanistan in the 1980s. After the Soviets' defeat, he led the Taliban to control of Afghanistan in 1996. Under his leadership, the Taliban put in place a harsh version of Islamic law. Also in 1996, Omar's government allowed al-Qaeda to base its terrorist training camps in Afghanistan. Following the 9/11 attacks, Omar refused to hand bin Laden and other al-Qaeda leaders over for trial. Since the 2001 invasion of Afghanistan, Omar has been in hiding.

Mohamed Atta (1968–2001)

Mohamed Atta piloted American Airlines Flight 11 into the North Tower of the World Trade Center and is believed to have been the leader of the 9/11 hijackers. It is not known exactly when he joined al-Qaeda, but as a student in Hamburg, he became close with other young men who shared his views, including two others who also piloted planes on September 11. In 2000, Atta arrived in the United States to take flying lessons and prepare for the attacks.

Khalid Shaikh Mohammed (1965–)

Khalid Shaikh Mohammed was a wanted terrorist long before he joined al-Qaeda in 1998. In the mid–1990s, he worked with Ramzi Yousef—his nephew and the main terrorist responsible for the 1993 World Trade Center bombing—on plots to assassinate President Bill Clinton and blow up commercial airplanes. While on the run from U.S. authorities, he joined al-Qaeda. Mohammed was captured in Pakistan in 2003. Until 2006, he was held in secret CIA prisons. That year, he was moved to a U.S. prison in Guantanamo Bay, Cuba. At a 2006 hearing, Mohammed confessed to helping plan the 9/11 attacks.

GLOSSARY

air traffic controller A person who tells pilots when it is safe to take off and land and also monitors the routes of planes to prevent accidents.

allies People or countries that cooperate with each other. The term is often used to refer to countries that take military action together.

al-Qaeda The Islamist group led by Osama bin Laden that is responsible for the terrorist attacks of September 11, 2001, and many other acts of terrorism throughout the world. Its name means "the Base" in Arabic.

anthrax A type of bacteria that causes a deadly disease that attacks the lungs and skin.

beacon A device on an aircraft that gives out a signal that helps air-traffic controllers guide the craft.

bioterrorism Attacking people with germs, such as anthrax, to give them a disease.

bureaucratic Following a set of rules or procedures, especially within a large organization or government office.

cabinet A group of leaders of government agencies that advise the president or prime minister of a country.

carnage Bloodied bodies of those injured or killed by an attack.

chemical weapons Weapons made to harm people with chemicals, such as gases that damage or irritate the skin, when breathed in.

civil liberties The freedoms, such as those guaranteed by the U.S. Bill of Rights, that restrict the government from controlling or interfering in individuals' lives.

civil war A war between different groups within the same country.

coalition A group that agrees to work and act together to achieve the same agreed goal or outcome.

Cold War The period of political hostility between the United States and the Soviet Union after World War II in which the two superpowers competed for power by supporting and arming other countries.

command A base from which leaders—military or political—give orders.

communist A person who believes in a classless society in which the state controls wealth and ownership.

controversy Disagreement over an idea.

dictatorship A form of government in which a single ruler has total power over the rule of a country. Dictators usually gain this power through violence.

dirty bomb A terrorist weapon that spreads radioactive material through an explosion. It is not the same as a nuclear bomb, which can spread radioactive material for hundreds of miles. Any radiation spread by a dirty bomb would only cover a few blocks, or miles, of the explosion.

embassy A building in one country that is the headquarters of the ambassador from a foreign country.

evacuation The process of getting people out of a building or an area, usually when there is great danger.

fatwa A ruling on a point of Islamic law by a recognized religious authority.

financial markets Institutions for the trade of stocks and bonds.

friendly fire Gunfire that kills a member of one's own side.

grounded Forced or restricted to stay in a certain area.

hijack To take control of a vehicle, such as an airplane or a boat, by force and often for political purposes. Most hijackings aim to make the plane land somewhere other than its intended destination.

immigration Coming to live in a new country.

intelligence Information gathered about enemy activity.

Islamist A person who thinks government should be controlled by the laws of Islam.

jihad In Islam, it means a struggle fought as a religious duty.

Mace A chemical spray that disables people for a short time. It causes intense pain and discomfort to the eyes, and can also cause the victim to have trouble breathing. The effects can last between 30 minutes and two hours.

mayday The international distress call used by planes and ships.

mujahideen Islamic guerilla fighters.

NATO A political and military alliance formed after World War II which includes the United States, Britain, and other European allies.

Northern Alliance The name given to the remaining members of the Afghan regime that held power until 1995, when the Taliban took over.

pepper spray A spray that uses pepper to temporarily disable people by irritating the eyes, nose, throat, and skin.

press conference A gathering of reporters to hear a speech by a public figure. The press can usually ask questions after the speech.

public address system A system of speakers placed throughout a building so people can hear announcements. The speakers are usually used for fire drills or safety announcements.

Pulitzer Prize A prize given in the United States for achievement in literature, journalism, or music, funded by the estate of Joseph Pulitzer.

radar A system that uses radio waves to tell the locations of faraway objects. It is used to determine the speed, size, and location of ships and planes.

resolution A document expressing the official view of a group or government.

Secret Service A U.S. government agency that protects the president and other top officials.

Soviet Union The former communist country made up of Russia and fourteen other republics that existed between 1922 and 1991.

Taliban The name means "students of Islamic knowledge." Leaders of this political movement took over Afghanistan in 1996 and imposed a strict form of Islamic rule. They were removed from power in 2001 after a co-operative operation between the Northern Alliance and NATO.

telethon A long television program used to raise money for a particular cause.

terrorists People who use random or planned acts of violence to scare others into giving in to their political or financial demands.

transcontinental Traveling across a continent.

transponder A device in a plane that responds to radar by sending back a radio signal with identifying information.

vigil A peaceful demonstration, often at night, where candles are lit and speeches or prayers may be said. Vigils are often held in remembrance of someone or an event.

weapons of mass destruction Weapons designed to kill large numbers of people at one time, including biological, chemical, and nuclear weapons.

INDEX

ACKNOWLEDGMENTS

Please visit our web site at: **www.garethstevens.com**
For a free color catalog describing Gareth Stevens Publishing's list of high-quality books, call 1-800-542-2595 (USA) or 1-877-387-3178 (Canada). Gareth Stevens Publishing's fax: 1-877-542-2596

A copy of the Cataloging-in-Publication Data is available upon request from the publisher.

ISBN-10: 1-4339-0048-3   (lib. bdg.)
ISBN-13: 978-1-4339-0048-8   (lib. bdg.)

This North American edition first published in 2009 by
Gareth Stevens Publishing
A Weekly Reader® Company
1 Reader's Digest Road
Pleasantville, NY 10570-7000 USA

This U.S. edition copyright © 2009 by Gareth Stevens, Inc. Original edition copyright © 2008 ticktock Entertainment Ltd. First published in Great Britain in 2007 by ticktock Media Ltd., Unit 2, Orchard Business Centre, North Farm Road, Tunbridge Wells, Kent, TN2 3XF, U.K.

Gareth Stevens Executive Managing Editor: Lisa M. Herrington
Gareth Stevens Editors: Joann Jovinelly, Jennifer Magid-Schiller
Gareth Stevens Creative Director: Lisa Donovan
Gareth Stevens Designer: Giovanni Cipolla
Gareth Stevens Production Manager: Paul Bodley, Jr.
Gareth Stevens Publisher: Keith Garton

Photo credits: B=bottom; C=center; L=left; R=right; T=top
Sean Adair/Corbis: 5b, 11. AP/PA Photos: 43tl. Robert F. Bukaty/ AFP/Getty Images: 15t. Central Intelligence Agency: 41tl, 41bl. Consolidated News Pictures Inc/Rex Features: 23t. Corbis: OFCb, 19t, 20-21b, 22, 24t, 28br, 32-33c, 42tr. Federal Bureau of Investigation: 43tr, 43b. Fotos International/Rex Features: 4b. Getty Images: 5t, 12-13t, 15cr, 18bl, 18-19c, 20b, 24-25c, 33t. Stan Honda/AFP/Getty Images: 16-17c. Image from Heroes Comic Book on page 34b: ©2008 Marvel Characters, Inc. Used with permission. iStock: 4t. Doug Kanter/ AFP/Getty Images: 16. Pornchai Kittiwongsakul/AFP/Getty Images: 35t. KPA/Zuma/Rex Features: 41br. James Leynse/Corbis: 25t. Brennan Linsley/AFP/Getty Images: 30-31c. Georgi Nadezhdin/AFP/ Getty Images: 27b. NBC/Corbis: 9. Bernd Obermann/Corbis: 14t. Erik C Pendzich/Rex Features: 39tr. Rex Features: 6b, 20t, 23b, 28t, 28bl, 30t, 34b, 42tl, 42b. Bob Rowan; Progressive Image/Corbis: 32tl. Ron Sachs/Rex Features: 41tr. Shutterstock: 1, 2, 6-7tr, 7b, 7t, 8t, 8b, 12b, 13b, 17cr, 35b, 36tr, 36b, 37t, 37b, 40l, 48. Sipa Press/Rex Features: 5br, 17t, 26b, 27t, 29b, 38tl, 39b. STF/AFP/Getty Images: 31t. Charles Sykes/Rex Features: 18t. Mario Tama/Getty Images: OFCtl. Time & Life Pictures/Getty Images: 14b. Peter Turnley/Corbis: 15b, 38tr. Universal/Everett/Rex Features: 34t. US Airforce: 40r. Steve Wood/ Rex Features: 10.

Every effort has been made to trace the copyright holders. We apologize in advance for any unintentional ommisions. We would be pleased to insert the appropriate acknowledgments in any subsequent edition of this publication.

All rights reserved. No part of this book may be reproduced, stored in a retrieval system, or transmitted in any form or by any means, electronic, mechanical, photocopying, recording, or otherwise, without the prior written permission of the copyright holder. For permission, contact **permissions@gspub.com**.

Printed in the United States of America

1 2 3 4 5 6 7 8 9 10 10 09 08